FANNY WA

On Piano Teaching and Performing

FABER MUSIC

in association with

FABER & FABER

First published in 1983 by Faber Music Ltd
in association with Faber & Faber Ltd
3 Queen Square London WC1N 3AU
Printed in England by Halstan & Co Ltd

British Library Cataloguing in Publication Data

Waterman, Fanny
Fanny Waterman on piano teaching and performing.
1. Piano — Performance
I. Title
786.3'041 MT220

ISBN 0-571-10050-3

Contents

Other books by Fanny Waterman

(with Marion Harewood)

The Waterman/Harewood Piano Series:

Piano Lessons Book One – complete method for the beginner pianist

Piano Lessons Book Two

Piano Lessons Book Three

Piano Playtime Book One – very first solos and duets

Piano Playtime Book Two

Two at the Piano – 50 duets for young pianists

The Young Pianist's Repertoire Book One

The Young Pianist's Repertoire Book Two

Recital Repertoire Book One

Recital Repertoire Book Two – Sonatas and Sonatinas

(with Paul de Keyser)

The Young Violinist's Repertoire Book One

The Young Violinist's Repertoire Book Two

published by Faber Music Ltd, London

Preface

In 1978 I was invited by the Royal Society of Arts in London to give the Tolansky Memorial Lecture, and chose as my subject the preparation of the young pianist for the concert platform. The present book grew out of that lecture, stimulated in particular by a series of piano masterclass programmes I was commissioned to prepare for screening on TV Channel 4. In bringing the manuscript to press, I would like to acknowledge the invaluable help of my husband, Geoffrey de Keyser, and my publisher, Martin Kingsbury.

This book is dedicated to Geoffrey with gratitude and affection.

FANNY WATERMAN
July 1983

Introduction

In 1943 a 'brilliantly gifted pianist and musician' left the Royal College of Music, London, after studying with one of the finest teachers of the day. That student had won most of the important awards for pianists at the College and, at the end of her time there, she was invited to play at a Promenade Concert with Sir Henry Wood and the BBC Symphony Orchestra. What more auspicious beginning to a career as a concert pianist could there be?

Let me confess that I was that young pianist. As with so many young artists – the majority perhaps – things did not turn out quite as I expected. I found my vocation was teaching – my true vocation, that is, and not just second best to performing. I then began to ask myself how I could draw on my experience as a pianist to benefit others and to help them meet the challenges to be faced.

The three aspects of musical training which I believe to be of paramount importance are: learning to be a craftsman, learning to be a musician, and becoming an artist.

The first and most important step in becoming a fine pianist is to learn the craft, that is, to master every technical detail of piano playing by learning *how* to do it: how to play a scale at speed with each note of equal brilliance or pearly delicacy; to play trills and repeated notes dynamically controlled to suit the mood of the music; to develop a wrist staccato resembling the vertical action of a piston; to master the art of tone production and pedalling (the perpetual challenge of how to make the piano sing); to achieve powerful octaves, accurate skips, perfect co-ordination between the hands, balancing parts when playing more than one melody at once . . . all these and a host of other technical details.

Mastering such details will absorb the pianist from his first lesson to his last performance. Although work on problems of technique will occupy only a fraction of the pianist's working day (some being used simply for limbering up), it is nevertheless a vital part of his efforts to produce the most apt and beautiful sounds and convincing interpretations, which constitute the goal of all technical work. Craftsmanship or 'technique', cannot be created in a vacuum. I have never been able to accept that there is a dividing line between technique and the two other aspects of training – musicianship and artistry. With these we embrace a limitless and elusive field where each individual's imagination and personality have an essential role to play.

My approach is to help the pupil to explore the artistic essence of the work, and to strive for *his* ideal interpretation. No amount of 'technique' in the sense of a precise and faultless rendering of the notes, velocity, bravura, etc., will produce a fine interpretation. When my pupils play a passage accurately but without feeling, I tell them they sound like a musical typewriter. Only when practice is combined with study of the *meaning* of the music will it lead to an artistic performance.

So let us move to the second aspect of training – musicianship. From the beginning, every musician must learn how to shape and colour a phrase; then how to play it in relation both to the next phrase and to the previous phrase; how to join several phrases together rhythmically so that a large section, an exposition or development, for example, is fused together; and, finally, how to build together large sections to give the piece or movement rhythmic unity as one architectural whole. The teacher must help the young musician to do this by developing a strong rhythmic sense, getting him to play metronomically, so that even the shortest note is in its correct 'time-spot'. When his rhythmic understanding is secure, he must learn how to use rubato, where speeds fluctuate – almost imperceptibly in Classical music, more markedly with Romantic and contemporary composers. In acquiring musicianship, the study of style and knowledge of composers' lives and times, what instruments were used and how they sounded, is vitally important. The ability to phrase and 'time' stylishly reveals the fascinating differences between every performer, and marks each with his or her own individual stamp.

How can a pianist equipped with technical virtuosity and musical sensitivity blossom into an artist? This third and vital step is impossible to teach. Artistry is the one quality which, I believe, is innate, and therefore cannot be taught but only stimulated.

I shall return in more detail to these three aspects of studying the piano – craftsmanship, musicianship and artistry. But before doing this, it may be helpful if I outline my own lesson format.

Lesson format

Young beginners can only concentrate for a short time, so their lessons last approximately half an hour. Before introducing any new material, we will go through the previous week's work, with marks given for each item and an overall percentage. If they get 80% or over they get a blue star, 90% or over, a gold star. And ten lessons each with a star will win them a prize. I am a great believer in incentives. Better results can be obtained in this way than by telling an eight-year-old that if he practises every day, he *might* one day become a great pianist. On the other hand, I do emphasise that he must not pay too much attention to my marks, but great attention to my *re*marks. Special points for attention and a detailed plan for daily practice are always written down in a notebook. I also encourage a parent to be present at lessons. Parents then share the experience of the child, and in recalling the points raised at the lessons, can supervise practice at home and play a vital role in the child's progress and enjoyment of the piano. (I am sometimes asked how I choose my pupils, and I reply: ideally I don't choose the pupils, I choose the parents!)

At the first lesson I give the young pianist Ten Musical Commandments. These vary somewhat according to his age and capability, but the principal ones are as follows: (1) Keep your back straight and your fingers rounded; (2) Practise regularly every day; (3) Before you start playing any unfamiliar music, clap the rhythm counting the beats aloud; (4) Choose fingering most suited to your hand, write it on the music and keep to it; (5) Hands separate before hands together; (6) Practise slowly before playing up to speed; (7)

When practising, correct any mistake immediately and play the passage several times correctly before going on or back; (8) Play any piece with precise rhythm throughout before introducing any rubato or rhythmic freedom; (9) Follow *all* the composer's markings; (10) Listen to *every* sound you make on the piano.

The normal lesson time for older children is about one hour. This gives time for technical work – Czerny studies, for example, and basic exercises which I have evolved over the years – one or two pieces in different styles, sight reading and aural tests. Each piece will give rise to technical work on such details as fingering, tone-production and phrasing. One or two pieces are studied in great depth over a period of many weeks in preparation for a performance – I believe that a piece is not really learnt until it has been performed either in public or to family and friends at home. The teacher should always look for opportunities to arrange informal concerts in front of other young musicians and their parents, since these provide a valuable stimulus and incentive.

Advanced students are encouraged to listen to each others' lessons, which last one or two hours (or indeed more) depending on the amount of work prepared. I rarely work on pre-prepared exercises, scales or studies in these lessons, but I do concentrate on any technical problems that arise in the course of the lesson. The student brings a piece of his own choice: it is important that he plays something for which he has a natural love and affinity. I may, of course, offer suggestions as to what he should learn next, in order to help him build a balanced repertoire from which he can later choose recital programmes.

At the beginning of every lesson the student will play a whole piece or movement without interruption, and from memory. Whatever mishaps occur he must carry on – for he must learn quickly to cover up mistakes and recover from memory slips. This is, of course, quite the reverse of his reaction to making mistakes when practising at home. Then he must stop, recall exactly what happened, think critically why the mistake was made, correct it, play the correct version several times, and only then link the entire passage with what follows. (A tape recorder can be invaluable for exposing both a technical fault and the factors which lead to it.) It is said that if Toscanini's players didn't deliver at a rehearsal he would explode; but if there was a slip-up at a performance, this was the human factor: it could happen to anyone at any time and there were never any post-mortem recriminations.

Memorising is, I believe, something everyone can do if it is tackled in the correct way – unlike, for example, sight-reading, for which some pianists have a natural flair. First, there is the tactile sense by which the pianist absorbs a specific fingering pattern over a period of weeks. Then there is the photographic memory: knowing that on the score, on the top left-hand side, for example, is the 'end of the second subject'. Seeing this in his mind's eye the pianist can, as it were, turn over the pages in his imagination as he is playing. Then there is the aural memorising – knowing what sounds follow next and how to find them on the keyboard. I never say to my pupils 'Memorize this piece by next week', because memorizing should not be forced but come naturally out of the concentrated effort that is required in studying any piece. Of course, one must be very careful when one alters fingering: it shouldn't be the day before a recital! It takes some time to absorb new fingering, and one must take into account the sense of stress which generally occurs before a performance in public.

When the student is playing at his lesson I will follow the score, and will be making notes and comments in it. I insist on good editions with as little editing as possible, although it is always interesting to examine the editions of masters such as Schnabel (his edition of the Beethoven Sonatas) or Cortot (Chopin's *Etudes*). At the end of the student's performance, I will always find something to praise and then make general critical comments. The real work then begins, on *every* note of *every* phrase in the greatest detail. The student must be able to start from any beat of any bar (eventually from memory). The opening phrase of a piece could absorb an entire lesson – for instance, the first chord of Beethoven's Fourth Piano Concerto, or the precise rhythmic pattern in the pianissimo opening of his 'Appassionata' Sonata, or the relationship of sound and silence in the first bars of Liszt's B minor Sonata.

I will try the passage myself several times in different ways, and together the student and I discover the approach he likes best. He, in turn, will try the passage several times and the process of exploration and discovery is continued until *he* has clarified his interpretation for himself. These reciprocal exchanges may go on for some time. As part of the process of exploration, I will comment on details such as the balance between the hands, singing the top note of a chord, polyphonic clarity, the unobtrusive emergence of one chord from another, the mood of the passage, and so on. Besides playing, I will also demonstrate by singing, conducting, explaining, making up words to fit the music, capturing its mood with a quotation from a piece of poetry, even dancing, if necessary. The process is applied to successive passages until we have covered the entire piece or movement and a unified performance has emerged.

I must now return to the first aspect of musical training – craftsmanship or 'technique' – in greater detail.

Craftsmanship

Technical development and musical development should go hand in hand – a great painter, an actor, a doctor, scientist or composer must know 'how to', and this is where technique begins.

No two hands, as the police well know, are the same. In the early stages of learning the piano, great thought must be given to the most comfortable fingering of a passage, with the proviso that it also produces the best sound. Pupils, I find, all too readily accept the 'ready-made' fingering printed in their music. If they do so, I will ask them how well they remember the hand of, say, Mr Harold Craxton. Did he have long slender fingers or short chubby ones? They give me a blank stare in reply, until I point out to them that the fingering has been done by Harold Craxton to suit *his* hand, and he certainly had quite a different hand from theirs. Their fingering must be 'made to measure' and worked out with the help of the teacher. To show the pupil how hands and fingers vary in size and shape, the teacher should trace in pencil the outline of his own hand and the pupil's on a sheet of paper or inside the cover of his music, and compare the two.

Craftsmanship must start with tone-production. Even on a single note we can play from the softest to the loudest sound; we can produce a large tone without hardness and a pianissimo that will carry to the last row of the top gallery. I like to explain this tonal variety to my pupils by comparing it to the artist's palette of colours. Just as there are many different shades of blue – for example, powder blue, turquoise, navy blue, sky blue, wedgwood blue and pacific blue – so there are many different nuances of piano tone. Much has been written and said about tone-production and I would like initially to draw attention to a few important considerations.

First, the pianist must learn how to listen to himself – how really to listen, that is, to the quality of every sound he produces. Good tone-production comes, in the first place, from having the right sound in your mind so that you can recognize it when you hear it. The teacher can help by demonstrating at the piano the range of possibilities, and by constantly encouraging the student to assess whether a particular sound he is producing matches the sound he is aiming for. When he has once heard himself produce a really fine tone, he will never forget it. I sometimes ask my pupils whether they would rather hear an indifferent pianist on a good piano or a good pianist on an indifferent instrument. I remind them that, unlike other instrumentalists, a pianist cannot carry his own piano around with him. But he can carry his own sound with him by his ability to cajole that sound out of even an indifferent instrument. (Sometimes he may find himself having to play on a piano that is worse than indifferent, in which case I tell him to do the best he can: 'What can't be cured must be endured'.)

This leads on directly to the second element in tone-production, the question of 'touch'. It is vital for the pianist to understand that the character and volume of sound depends on the speed at which the piano key descends. To control the speed of key descent is to control the volume. It is also to control the tonal colour, since the 'mix' of partials caused by a forcible impact of hammer on string is different from that produced by a gentler one. I show my pupils that the key can be depressed by only a quarter of an inch, and that all types of tone must be produced within this small depth.

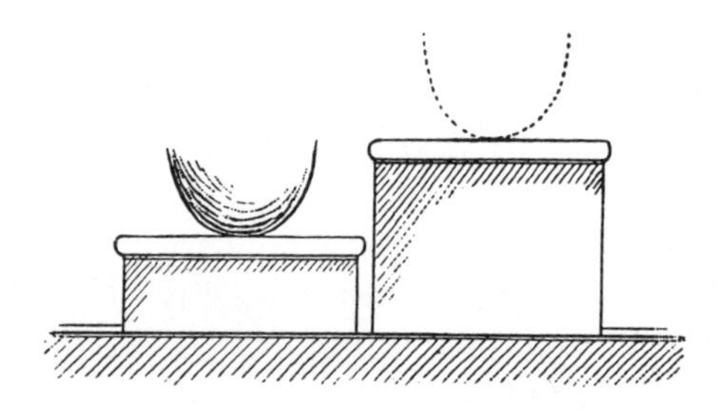

If the key is depressed very slowly, no sound at all is emitted. By quickening the descent just fractionally, the thinnest thread of sound can be produced. The pianist must feel the exact finger movement required, which of course will vary from one piano to another. At the other extreme the hand can come swiftly down on the key from a height to produce a really full, strong sonority. Between these extremes come the many speeds of descent which yield the full palette of tonal colours.

To make the point clear to my younger pupils, I ask them to imagine that they have a rubber ball in their hand. If it slips gently down to the ground, it will produce much less noise than if it were bounced with vigour. They soon get the message, and enjoy producing sounds at different dynamic levels and in the differing moods associated with each level. This is exploited in one of the first five-finger tunes I give to beginners (see opposite).

Tone quality is, of course, also affected by the position of the fingers. Bright passage-work requires well rounded fingers (joints well bent), so that only the fingertips are in contact with the keys. For fuller tone, the fingers must be less rounded, i.e. slightly flatter (joints less bent), so that the fleshy

LULLABY

If you play this softly and die away at the end, it will sound like a lullaby.

MARCH

If you play this loudly and finish with a bold ending, it will sound like a march.

cushion of the fingertip is used. This can be demonstrated by tapping a table first with the tip of a pencil and then with the flat of its full length; also try playing imaginary notes on your bare arm – first with the fingertips (well rounded fingers), then with the fleshy cushion of the fingertips (fingers flatter) – so that you can feel the difference.

The use of the sustaining pedal is an important element in tone-production, and I will come to this later in this section.

The last general point concerns the wrist. A stiff, tense wrist is enemy number one, and will inhibit any good tone-production. On the other hand, a flexible wrist acts as a shock-absorber. In full tone it allows the weight of the arm to be transmitted to the fingers without the percussive bumps and thumps that otherwise are so frequently produced. In fast passage-work it should not be too yielding, but through its flexibility gives essential elastic support to the fingers. Of course, the wrist will never be flexible if the arm and shoulder are tense. So it is equally important that the arm is relaxed and the shoulder down, never hunched.

Before tackling any passage-work, we must learn to play two connected notes with the same power and evenness, backwards and forwards in a see-saw movement, transferring the weight from one finger to another, keeping the arm relaxed and the shoulder down (see the See-Saw Exercise below). We should always play on the tips of the fingers (nails short – yes, even the girls!), and keep the fingers rounded, with the joints well bent. If I find any tendency towards straightening the fingers, I ask the pupil to try running with straight legs – the point is quickly made.

SEE-SAW EXERCISE

The same principles should be applied to more extended 3, 4 and 5-finger exercises – there are many studies of Czerny for this purpose. We must learn to grade the tone from *pp* to *ff*, to play both slowly and quickly, legato and staccato. All fingers should be placed in the middle of each key; this helps, right from the beginning, to avoid split notes. It is important to give the weakest 4th finger special attention or it will produce a limp sound in comparison with the stronger fingers, especially the thumb and the 3rd finger. The pupil should try playing a scale up and down the piano as legato as possible, using the 3rd and 4th fingers, then the 4th alone. The secret is to keep the knuckles arched, to raise the fingers as little as possible in moving from note to note, and not to raise the arm at all. Make sure there is no stiffening in the arm or the shoulder.

We should note, in passing, that the 4th finger's lack of independence stems from the fact that its tendons have connections with those of its two adjoining fingers. We therefore have less muscular control over that specific finger. (Though it is unlikely that the cradle devised by Schumann was the primary cause of his celebrated problems with the 4th finger, we should take heed and not allow exercises to continue in a condition of strain.)

In approaching passage-work and scales, we must be conscious of the relative nature of speed and time. In everyday life a second is the shortest space of time in general use. But musicians must train themselves to think in fractions of a second – a half, a quarter, an eighth, even a sixteenth of a second. A scale played with a note per second will sound slow. Played twice as fast (each note half a second), it is still too slow for most passage-work. Played twice as fast again (each note a quarter of a second), it is at a moderate speed. Halve the time again, and we have now arrived at the approximate speed of the semiquavers/sixteenth-notes in a Mozart Allegro. There is still the possibility of halving the time yet again to produce timings of a sixteenth of a second and even shorter, the kind of split-second timings that every musician must eventually master and control in his playing.

One of the chief difficulties occurring in passage-work and scales is, of course, the passage of the thumb under the hand (ascending in the right hand, descending in the left) and the passage of the hand over the thumb (descending in the right hand, ascending in the left). The thumb enjoys more muscular power and freedom of movement than any of the fingers. It not only can move in the opposite direction to them but also functions as a pivot on which the hand can move laterally in either direction. These facilities are exploited in the thumb exercises I give my pupils, in the key of each of the scales they learn. In these exercises, holding the elbow against the side of the body helps to prevent the arm jutting out sideways each time the thumb passes under the hand.

THUMB EXERCISES

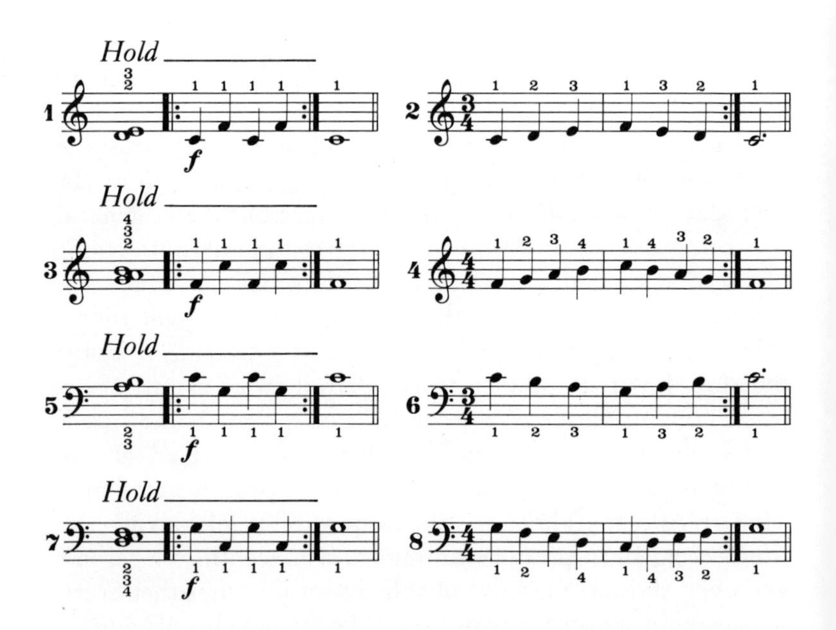

There are very few complete ascending and descending scales in the great works we study. Yes – the opening of Beethoven's Third Piano Concerto has three ascending scales, and Chopin's Prelude in B flat minor Op 28 No 16 has complete or nearly complete scales in almost all of its 46 bars. But, on the whole, we have to play *fragments* of scales.

Breaking up scales into fragments, both note by note and beat by beat, is therefore a valuable exercise:

BREAKING UP

(a) Note by note:

(b) Beat by beat:

The same technique can be applied to each successive degree of the scale, using the 'key-note' fingerings. Another useful exercise is to play scales in different rhythms and with different dynamics: soft and *leggiero*, loud and *con brio*, starting *f* and getting softer, starting *p* and getting louder, and so on.[1]

The value of such an approach to scales is twofold: the student is introduced to differing types of passage-work he will find in the pieces he studies, and at the same time he is provided with models for practising those problematic passages he encounters and will have to master. I think that the formal practising of scales for their own sake has little value and can, indeed, having a numbing effect on students' concentration and listening capacity. They would do better to

[1] These are set out in the Appendix in *Piano Lessons Book Two* and *Book Three.*

spend their time in extending their repertoire and applying the 'breaking-up' technique to the fast passage-work in the pieces they learn. It is always helpful to think of such passages as slow melodies played fast, and for this reason I encourage students to sing quick passages slowly so as to focus their hearing on each note in turn.

Similar considerations apply to arpeggios and broken chords. The secret here is not to attempt to prepare too many notes in advance. The student should aim for evenness of tone, keeping his wrists flexible and free to move laterally. To help him get the feel of the different distances of different intervals, he should put the thumb note down silently and play aloud the notes on either side of it – each with its correct fingering. Once again, holding the elbow against the side helps to prevent the arm from jerkily jutting out each time the thumb passes under the hand. There are a number of Czerny studies to help pupils with this problem, while for advanced students the Chopin Study Op 10 No 1 is excellent.

I referred earlier to trills, which in my experience always require special attention. In the first place, a trill must consist of two separate notes, not one blurred sound. The see-saw two-note exercise is the one to practise here, slowly at first and then building up the speed. Vary the fingering by using 1st and 2nd, 2nd and 3rd and so on, first on adjacent black notes, then on adjacent white notes, then on adjacent black and white notes. Play also at different dynamic levels and then introduce crescendos and diminuendos. Finally, as the trill progresses, vary the speed. Differing combinations of these elements will be required in differing musical contexts – from the bravura of the final bars of a Concerto cadenza to the dream-like quality of a slow Chopin Nocturne. Practising with a metronome helps to keep trills rhythmic – and the breaking-up method is as vital here as with scales. As so often in piano playing, singing the written notes is also helpful to establish their relationship with each other and reveal their melodic content. Ends of trills frequently evaporate in a melée of mush. The remedy is to start on the previous beat and play to the last note of the bar – *not* the first note of the next bar – and wait there, listening to check that the hands are still exactly together. When a trill is accompanied by an Alberti bass, there is often a tendency to accent the principal beats too strongly, so care must be taken to avoid such over-accentuation.

Another technical matter I should mention is the acquisition of a good octave technique, since this writing occurs so much in the piano repertoire, thickening the bass and providing a solid foundation, or adding steely brilliance to the treble. (Octaves in the lower register have a particularly important function in that their upper partials reinforce the treble by adding increased resonance.) A pianist with large hands can take octaves in his stride, so long as the wrists remain loose but the fingertips are firm. For accuracy in octave playing the student should practise with the 5th finger alone, and with the thumb alone. For those with small hands, I stress the importance of stretching exercises every day of their lives – without overdoing it, of course. Even the smallest increase in the extension of their hand will help prevent tightening up and give them a large increase in the repertoire they can tackle. The following exercises I have found helpful and each teacher can work out further examples:

STRETCHING EXERCISES

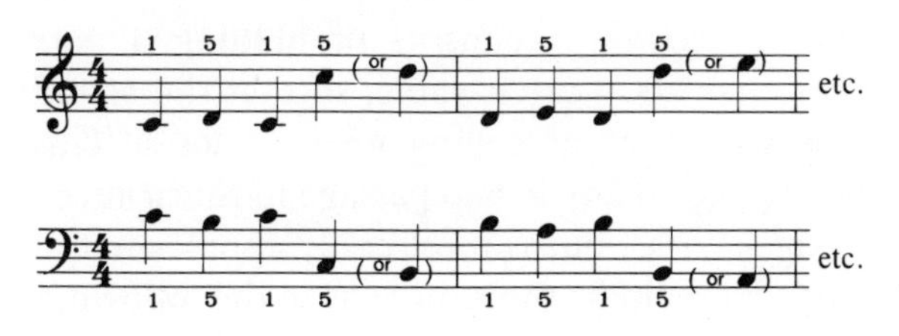

Another technical problem arises over skips. A student may play a difficult skip for hours and it will barely improve; encourage him to use his brains, however, and it is easily improved. I point out that a wide skip involves moving your whole arm, and only if you move it as quickly as possible just above the keys can you arrive in time to play at the other end. But I would go one better than punctuality: if you have to reach notes at the top of the piano, and your journey starts at the bottom, get there *before* you're due. (Nelson attributed whatever success he had in life to his habit of arriving half an hour early for every appointment.) This means practising moving your arm as quickly as you can to the position required for the next notes – but don't play them; that's a waste of time at the moment. Just check that the fingers are above the correct notes. Then, with any luck, at the next attempt you will master the leap straight off.

We now come to the most difficult problem facing the pianist – how to make a primarily percussive instrument 'sing'. Three possible techniques are:

1. Intentional overlapping of notes in a melody;
2. Adjusting the balance of tone between different parts – between melody and accompaniment, between the voices in contrapuntal writing, and so on;
3. Using the sustaining pedal.

These three techniques are not, of course, mutually exclusive and can be exploited simultaneously. Let us briefly consider each of them.

The overlapping technique consists of holding a note fractionally longer than its written value, so that the sound minutely overlaps with the succeeding note or notes. This technique can be applied to any legato passage in music (even scales or fast passage-work), but is most easily appreciated in and applied to disjunct melodic movement as in the following example:

Play:

Then remove the pauses and shorten the second of each pair of tied notes so that only a fractional overlap occurs. Split-second timing is here the secret of welding the sounds together and of producing in this way even, cantabile tone.

Split-second timing is similarly required to achieve the differentiated syntheses of sounds which are the essence of 'balance'. This works in two ways. First, as we saw earlier, the speed and weight with which the piano key is depressed determines the character and volume of the sound. Balancing the tone, either between the two hands or between principal and subsidiary notes played by a single hand, is therefore a function of the speed of key descent. But it is also a matter of differential timing, in that any note gains prominence if played fractionally before other notes sounded with it. One way of achieving this is to straighten very slightly the finger playing the melody note, while keeping the other fingers well bent. I need hardly say that this trick of the trade must be handled with great discretion and must never be exaggerated – we are really talking about micro-seconds – but the technique is particularly useful to bring out and sustain one or more parts in contrapuntal music or a melodic line in chordal textures.

Take, for example, a three-part invention. One can bring out the middle part by playing every note fractionally before the top part, so that whenever the sounds coincide, the middle

RIGHT-HAND BALANCE

BALANCE BETWEEN HANDS

part will have the first aural impact on the listener. Then, if one plays the top part *louder* than the middle part, one will be able to bring that out as well. The beauty of it is that, having dealt in this way with two parts, the third assumes an identity of its own, if only by its apparent subservience to the other two. Such an approach can lead to the clarity of articulation required in all contrapuntal music from Bach to Liszt and on into the twentieth-century repertoire.

Tchaikovsky's *Chorus* from his Children's Album Op 39 (see opposite) provides an example of a melodic line that must emerge from a chordal texture. The opening chords can be practised as indicated.

The sustaining pedal is one of the piano's greatest assets (Chopin called it 'the soul of the piano'). Yet its use is so subtle that it is one of the most difficult techniques to teach and to master.

We must first be aware that the sustaining pedal not only prolongs the sound of a note and allows successive notes to be joined through their overlapping with each other; it also enriches the sound by adding an aura of harmonics and thus places at the player's disposal an important means of colouring the tone.

The mechanism is familiar enough. Normally all strings are damped, and only those being struck by the hammers, as the keys are depressed, are temporarily free of the dampers. With the sustaining pedal depressed, all the dampers are raised, and therefore all the strings are able to vibrate freely. When a note is now struck, its upper partials (i.e. the harmonic series) are reinforced as the strings concerned vibrate in sympathy and thereby add their resonance to the fundamental. It is for this reason that the pedal is sometimes called the 'loud' or 'forte' pedal.

The player can control the amount of resonance of any note or chord – and thus its tone quality and carrying power – by his timing in depressing and raising the pedal. The greatest resonance is obtained when the pedal is depressed before a note or chord is struck. When it is depressed simultaneously with the keys, the sound is still full but somewhat less sonorous. This is useful for giving resonance to the first note of a phrase, or to detached notes or chords; and in these cases it is important to remember that, just as the pedal goes *down* at the same moment as the fingers, it must also come *up* simultaneously with the fingers, or very nearly so.

The most common type of pedalling is 'syncopated' pedalling. Here the pedal is depressed fractionally after the keys and is raised immediately a new note or chord begins to sound, at which point the process may be repeated. The split-second overlapping of sounds that result from this type of pedalling produces a legato effect similiar to that obtained by the 'overlapping' technique using only the fingers as earlier described. But we must never forget that the pedal is a far more potent mechanism than the fingers for sustaining sounds. The two elements must always be carefully co-ordinated. Excellent finger-work can all too easily be wrecked by inefficient or over-enthusiastic pedalling.

This is especially true in the lower registers of the piano, since the lower the note, the greater the effect of the pedal will be. In general terms, the pedal can be depressed earlier and for a longer period for notes in the high register than for those in the middle and low registers, without the sounds becoming obtrusive or blurring with each other. The acoustics of the instrument, as well as those of the hall, will be a decisive factor in determining the minute differences in timing that are required.

It is, of course, possible and sometimes desirable to pedal through a group of notes, provided this does not interfere with a change of harmony or the ending of a phrase. In passage-work, for example, we can greatly enhance the flow of the line by giving a dab of pedal at the peak of a phrase.

Rhythmic pedalling on the beat is always to be avoided in this context, but in sequential passages selective pedalling through a group of notes, varying the choice from one sequence to the next, can be particularly effective. Discreet pedalling can also usefully assist a gradual crescendo in both loud and soft passages. However, the pedal should never be held down through rests or staccato notes unless for special effects. Remember too that the total absence of pedal in a passage is in itself often a striking effect.

Beyond such generalities, the use of the pedal will always be highly subjective. In much Romantic and later music it is clearly a necessary ingredient for both technical and interpretative reasons, even where its use has not been specifically marked by the composer. Without the sustaining pedal one simply cannot achieve the luminous quality of sound required in a Chopin Nocturne or the impressionistic sense of *'Dans une brume doucement sonore'* called for by Debussy in his prelude *La Cathédrale engloutie*. In Classical and earlier music it is a valuable means of colouring and sustaining the tone, in other words making the piano 'sing'. However for legato playing in such music, my own preference is to rely primarily on finger-work ('overlapping' and 'balancing' techniques), with the pedal as a helpful adjunct. One must beware, incidentally, of composers' own pedal markings in some 18th-century music. They were valid for the instruments of the time when the pedal had only recently been introduced, but are not always to be taken literally on the much more resonant instruments of today.

One word about foot technique. While the heel rests on the floor, taking the weight of the leg, the ball of the foot should remain in constant contact with the pedal. The pedal is normally depressed swiftly but without using too much force – certainly without stamping. When allowed to rise, it must always rise sufficiently for the dampers to make full contact with the strings. In syncopated pedalling the rise is quick and the damping sudden. But one can also allow the pedal to rise more slowly so that the damping is gradual, as in the case of a long held note or chord. The term 'half-pedalling' is often applied to the technique of partial damping, when the depressed pedal is allowed to rise momentarily and insufficiently for the dampers to be fully effective. Correctly used, this technique will allow a bass note struck once to continue sounding, while notes in the upper register – moving chords, for example, played by both hands – are damped. Sustained 'pedal points' can, of course, be obtained more efficiently and in any register by the use of the middle or sostenuto pedal, when a piano is fitted with this useful device.

To end this section on craftsmanship, here are some words of wisdom for practising:

Bacon said 'A lame man on the right road arrives sooner than a fast runner on the wrong one'.

Stephen Heller said 'Practise very slowly, progress very fast'; one might add 'Practise very fast, progress very slowly'.

Musicianship

Now to return to the second aspect of training – learning to become a fine musician.

When a composer writes a piece of music, he gives us not only the notes, but also some clues as to how to play them. A musical pianist is a musical detective, able to spot all the clues. One of the first clues, though frequently overlooked, is the title. I have adjudicated at music festivals and discovered to my dismay that some competitors have not known the title of the piece they are playing. Or even if they knew the title – for example, a Mazurka – they did not know what a Mazurka is or what are its special characteristics. We should teach young pianists to investigate all the basic clues including the title, tempo indications, key signature, time signature, dynamics, phrase marks, accents, and silences (which are as important as sounds). They must learn how vital it is to follow and memorise the composer's markings; to ignore any one of them is to commit a musical crime. Of course, it is a feat to memorize every marking, but if the student has what I call 'musical integrity' he will remember everything down to the last staccato dot – particularly in Beethoven and Brahms who were so painstaking in their phrasing and dynamic markings.

All players are entrusted with the works composers have written for their instruments. It is as if they have personally received a legacy under each composer's will: Beethoven's 32 Sonatas, Chopin's 4 Ballades and Bach's 48 Preludes and Fugues – to name but three examples – are the priceless inheritance of everyone who plays the piano. That inheritance carries with it a responsibility to the composer, and a further responsibility to the audience. Only through his musical integrity can the pianist fulfil that dual responsibility in his re-creation of these great works of art.

Of course, there will always be the problem of interpreting the shorthand of musical notation. It is impossible to define exactly how slow is *adagio,* how leisurely is an *andante,* or how much faster *più allegro* should be than the preceding *allegro.* (I tell my pupils 'How much *più* is up to you'.) It is equally impossible to define exactly how soft is *piano,* how loud is *forte,* how much emphasis to put on a *sfortzato.* Great thought must be given to these tempi indications and dynamics, their sonorities and textures. The same dynamic produces a different quality of sound in the different registers of the keyboard. Children love the story of the Three Bears when you tell it using three different registers of voice: 'And Father said [in a very deep voice], "Who's been eating my porridge?"; Mother said [in a higher voice], "Who's been eating my porridge?"; and Baby Bear said [in a high, shrill voice], "Who's been eating my porridge, and eaten it all up?" And it is the same on the piano, as we can demonstrate, where each register has a different timbre.

I encourage my pupils to compare these different timbres to those of the orchestra: piano sound in a low register resembles the tone of a double bass or cello and is richer than the viola tone of the middle register or the ringing tone of the violin-like high register. Indeed, a pianist should sometimes imagine the piano to be an orchestra, and sonatas to be symphonies. He should try to imitate the sounds of different instruments. Beethoven Sonatas are full of quartet writing (the E major Sonata Op 14 No 1, for example, which Beethoven himself arranged as a string quartet). Bülow, in his edition of Beethoven's Sonatas, marks passages 'Quasi Clarionet', 'Quasi Horn', and used to advise pupils to imitate Joachim's violin tone. Or we can think of vocal timbre: in several of the slow movements of Mozart's Piano Concertos, the melody line is like an expressive Aria.

Music cannot exist without melody. It is essentially Song and the art of singing has influenced composers from the lullaby of the cradle to the elegy of the grave. To play a simple melody with fine tone and rhythm is one of the greatest of our pianistic challenges. Compare a melody to a sentence in speech – not every word is equally important, and only the most meaningful words are emphasised. A speaker can alter the meaning of a sentence by his choice of emphasis: 'To be or not to be' – even so short a phrase takes on different shades of meaning according to his timing and the degree of emphasis placed on key words. So too a musician can alter the meaning of a musical phrase. Consciously or unconsciously, he must be aware of many of its characteristics: which is the lowest note and which the highest; which are the shortest notes and which the longest; does it progress in steps (conjunct motion) or in leaps (disjunct motion); are notes repeated and, if so, for what expressive purpose? Equally he must be aware of the position and importance of the phrase within the larger melodic span.

In comparing a melody to a sentence or line of poetry, I tell students that, as with words, notes must flow – 'like oil', as Mozart said. But, in order to make sense, the punctuation must also be carefully observed. Here is a sentence without any punctuation:

King Charles walked and talked half an hour after his head was cut off.

Now, the same words, with punctuation:

King Charles walked and talked. Half an hour after, his head was cut off.

Music must also make sense. Without properly punctuated phrasing, music is just as nonsensical as the unpunctuated sentence about King Charles. Musicians, in fact, tend to use far too many full-stops in their playing, where only commas and semi-colons are necessary. Their understanding of phrasing can be helped considerably by a theoretical knowledge of musical forms, of harmony and of rhythmic structures, together with aural training.

Just as sentences contain key words, so each melody has a climax – though different artists will naturally have different views on exactly where it should be. Pianists must learn always to play rhythmically forward towards the climax, and never stand still, even in a rest or a pause. (Finality comes only with the silence at the end of a piece.) And having shaped a melody, the pianist must then make sure that it is balanced with the accompaniment so that it gets the necessary – yet unobtrusive – support. Finally, having gone through all these details with blood, sweat and toil, his performance should still sound uncontrived.

Music is an art fraught with temporal problems. Not only must the pianist always think ahead, but he can perform in the present only in relationship to what has happened in the past and what is about to happen in the future. This thought process must not only be applied to short passages, but must be used to give continuity to large sections of a piece. In a sonata movement, for example, the pianist must make sure that there are no seams showing between the first and second subjects (a radical change in tempo is always to be avoided). Then, the development must *be* a development, with its exciting modulations and bigger tonal proportions. And after the recapitulation, the coda must take its due place as the climax of the movement, perhaps, or as a tranquil memory with a tonal level to match. This is what I meant when I referred in the Introduction to the need to give each piece 'rhythmic unity as one architectural whole'.

In a performance, we must imagine that we are going on a journey in time. We should know our destination, but also be aware of the delights and surprises on the way. It can be a long journey, as in Schubert's D major Sonata, or a short journey, as in a Chopin Prelude. We can go slowly, as in a Brahms Intermezzo, or run quickly, as in a spirited Scarlatti Sonata. But, whatever the music, we must always keep on moving forward, tonally and rhythmically, and not mark time on one spot or stop.

A metronome can be useful to set a speed; it also strengthens the rhythm, and prevents running away in quick passages or dragging in slow. There is a game I play with my pupils which shows the difficulty of maintaining a metronomically strict tempo. While I play the opening of a rhythmic piece – say, a March – two pupils, standing back to back, conduct in time to my playing. I then stop playing and they both continue conducting on their own. After a short time they turn round and compare the correlation of their beats: the chance is only a hundred to one that they will still be together.

When we play, we must be aware simultaneously of the basic pulse and of the rhythmic patterns into which it is divided. It would be wonderful if we could have built into our physiques a number of timing devices to cope with complicated and simultaneous rhythmic patterns. This would be a great improvement on Maelzel's metronome, which can only give us regular beats, and which can easily make us play mechanically.

What constitutes a good rhythmic performance? There must be a certain regularity of pulse; on the other hand, a relentless, metronomic observance of the beat would destroy the living rhythm, as would any artificial deviation from it. Matthay said that rhythm should be bent but not broken. We must encourage students to aim for a buoyant springiness of timing, but without unnecessary liberties. There must always be a reason and purpose behind the slight accelerandos and ritardandos which we call rubato. The rise and fall of intervals in a melody, for example; the magic of an unexpected harmony; the building up of a climax or the repose of a final statement in the coda of a slow movement – rhythmic licence in such contexts can never be expressed accurately by notation or tempo indication. No two artists can ever perform the same composition in the same way, and I doubt if a performer ever gives exactly the same performance twice over.

This is not to say that composers' tempo indications are not of vital importance. Beethoven made up for the lack of performing instructions in 18th-century music by making his tempo indications more and more specific. He went in for markings like *Nicht zu geschwind und sehr singbar vorzutragen* (Non troppo vivace e cantabile assai). I strongly advise my pupils to think carefully about these markings, and never to imitate other performers' ideas from a gramophone record which never changes. When a student has studied a work in depth, then I encourage him to listen to as many live performances as possible. One must never, however, ape another artist. Some young musicians today, instead of studying the score in the minutest detail and re-creating the music for themselves, give performances which are a hotch-potch of ideas thrown together from recordings of every pianist under the sun. Beethoven would never have approved of such a method of 'instant' learning. He was such a stickler for detail that, after reprimanding his pupil Czerny for not following the music, he had to apologise the next day: 'You must forgive a composer who would rather have his work performed exactly as it was written, however beautifully you played it in *other* respects'.

Our lives are governed by rhythm – from a watch ticking away the seconds to the 24-hour rhythm of night and day. Somewhere in between is the fundamental rhythm of our heart-beat. It is surely not a coincidence that the normal heart rate of 60-80 pulses per minute is the speed so often chosen by composers for their works. We hear rhythmic patterns every day of our lives – the ticking of a clock, which groups itself into two's, three's or four's, making duple, triple or quadruple time at the listener's will; the telephone bell; windscreen-wipers; galloping horses; the steady dripping of a tap. In music, this grouping of beats forms bars and each group of these forms a phrase; phrases join together to form larger sections such as exposition, development or recapitulation, until the entire movement or work can be seen as a whole, like the panoramic but detailed view from an aeroplane as it comes into land.

Sometimes the bar-lines are important guide-lines, when it is necessary to reveal the recurring first beat of a bar, but sometimes their function is only visual and they must be mentally erased in favour of a more natural and longer flow of rhythmic line.

Each small rhythmic pattern must be learnt precisely from the very beginning of one's musical training. The exact proportions of, for example, a minim and two crotchets (half-note and two quarter-notes) or of a crotchet and two quavers (quarter-note and two eighth-notes) are not in themselves problematic and can be clapped with precision. When the same rhythm is transferred to the keyboard, however, the very mechanics of finger-work create difficulties for the unwary. The result is a surprisingly frequent and widespread incidence of unrhythmical playing, which in turn destroys the expressive content of the music.

Take, for example, the opening of Schubert's 'Wanderer' Fantasy. If the crotchet/quarter-note is shortened here, the first of the two quavers/eighth-notes will be sounded earlier than it should and thus attract an unwanted accent, while the second quaver/eighth-note is lengthened in compensation. Such inaccurate rhythm will destroy the grandeur of the

passage. In fact, in almost all music rhythm is the skeleton on which the flesh of tonal colour and expression depend.

Dotted rhythms present another all-too-familiar trap. Take the opening of the famous Tchaikovsky Mazurka from his Children's Album Op 39. Here again tonal colour and rhythm are intimately connected. When the dotted rhythm is apportioned exactly three parts to one, the articulation will automatically be crisp and springy as required to express the spirit and style of the piece.

There are many other traps which the young performer must be warned against. Because of the natural decay of sound on the piano, longer notes as a general rule have to be played with more force than shorter ones. The tendency to hurry in quick passages should be countered by a sense of playing the notes with more control. (There is always a danger of panicking before a difficult passage. I tell my students 'Make haste slowly', i.e. to prepare and organize themselves before they come to the passage.) In a diminuendo passage, the piano keys will be depressed at a progressively slower rate in order to reduce the volume of sound and this all too frequently leads to a rallentando. The reverse occurs in a crescendo, when the player will naturally tend to hurry. We must also take into account that in a diminuendo there is often a gradual relaxation of tension, and in a crescendo the tension rises. Nicholas Moldavan, who played the viola in the Flonzale Quartet and was also a member of the NBC orchestra, described Toscanini's crescendos: 'Nobody could build up a crescendo as he did – by holding you back – holding you – holding you. Other conductors didn't know how to do that: they ran away with you: when it comes to the *forte* they haven't anything left. *He* knew how to build it up gradually.'

We have perhaps strayed away from musicianship into craftsmanship, but this in itself shows how ill-defined is the boundary between them. In practical terms, the pianist should be aware of fulfilling three roles when he plays:

1 The Performer – plays a few phrases.
2 The Listener – listens and stops to recall the sounds and silences he has produced.
3 The Critic – assesses and analyses the playing. Was it too loud, too soft, too quick, too slow? Did the tone, the rhythm, the musical punctuation and phrasing add up to his expressive intention?

In this context I cannot emphasise enough how important it is for the pianist to make his expressive intention, i.e. his interpretation, absolutely clear to the listener. A well-known American literary critic advised writers: 'Say what you mean; you will be taken to mean what you say'. Similarly any performer must recognise that a performance is the sum total of what he plays and that sum total is the message his audience will receive.

The teacher can always help the young pianist over the choice of repertoire. For beginners, we are fortunate to have such a large number of simple pieces by the great composers from which to choose – other instrumentalists are not so lucky. There are many short pieces by Handel in the Aylesford collection, and by Bach in the Anna Magdalena Notebook, the 20 short Preludes, and the two-and three-part Inventions. Then there are the pieces which Leopold Mozart collected for Nannerl and Amadeus and gave to them as presents on their name-day. There are also Amadeus Mozart's own short pieces, composed when he was very young. Schumann, Mendelssohn and Tchaikovsky all composed works specially for children and in the twentieth century we have simple pieces by Bartók, Kabalevsky and Shostakovich, to name but a few.

A detailed list of works for study and performance by more advanced students cannot be attempted here. The choice of a repertoire, and the selection of works for a recital programme will depend as much on individual temperament as on technical ability and experience. However there are a few general points that should be made.

First, it is vital that pianists should be encouraged to study the masterworks of the Baroque period – Bach's Forty-Eight Preludes and Fugues, the Sonatas by Domenico Scarlatti, etc. The current orthodoxy is that such works should be played only on the instruments for which they were written and not on the modern piano. To follow such a 'purist' view is to deny the pianist an important and rewarding section of the greatest keyboard literature, which will also help his understanding of music written by later composers. Bach's 'Forty-Eight' have, after all, been called the Old Testament for pianists (Beethoven's Sonatas being the New Testament). Their contrapuntal style challenges the pianist to present the different voices with clarity, and with correct balance and expression. He can usefully imagine each part as an instrumental line in an orchestral score, as I mentioned earlier. The 'linear' thinking required in much Baroque music applies equally to many works of the Classical and

Romantic periods: it is not always appreciated that music by the Romantic composers is brimful of part-writing.

Within the huge Baroque repertoire, I would particularly recommend the Scarlatti Sonatas. There are over 500 to choose from – their emotional range is wider than is often realized, and they include practically every technical element a pianist has to master, from nimble passage-work to spectacular leaps and octaves.

The invention of the pianoforte or *Hammerklavier* in the 18th century inspired composers to exploit its new expressive possibilities. Its tone was at first small and intimate, less forceful in fact than the harpsichord and spinet which it only gradually replaced. In Haydn's Sonatas we can see the development of the Classical style in parallel with the demand for increasing volume and richer tone from the instruments on which the music was to be realized. His early sonatas are small in scale and intimate in character. As their formal construction grows more spacious, so too does the requirement for greater sonority and expression.

The rapid development of compositional style in the Classical period has an important consequence for the performer. The essential repertoire is wide enough – Haydn's Sonatas; Mozart's Rondos, Variations, Sonatas and Concertos; Beethoven's Bagatelles, Variations, Sonatas and Concertos. But to understand and perform even one sonata really well, it is essential to know many of them intimately. (This is a case of quantity yielding quality.) In Beethoven's case, for example, one must be familiar with sonatas from each of his three compositional periods in order to perform those particular sonatas with which one has a temperamental affinity. Incidentally, I do recommend Czerny's studies as an introduction to Beethoven, whose pupil he was. They capture the sound of Beethoven's passage-work and, for all we know, the style of his playing as well.

Familiarity with works in other genres is also helpful.

One must know Mozart's operas to play his Piano Concertos, Haydn's String Quartets to play his Sonatas, and Beethoven's Symphonies and String Quartets to play his Sonatas and Concertos.

Simultaneously with the Classical repertoire must come the study of the great Romantic composers: Schubert, Schumann, Chopin, Liszt and Brahms – their miniatures as well as their major works. Every student of the piano must learn the works of the Impressionist School of Fauré, Debussy and Ravel, for here is a unique world of sound, and then on to Bartók, Messiaen and other twentieth-century masters up to the present day.

Artistry and performance

When I go to a concert fresh, alert, and expectant, I sometimes find that, after a time, instead of listening to Beethoven's Op 110, or Chopin's Second Ballade, my mind is wandering on to other matters:

5 lbs of potatoes
2 lbs of carrots
2 lbs of onions
1 lb of tomatoes

I have focused on tomorrow's shopping expedition; try as I will, I cannot concentrate on the music, which passes over me and becomes incidental.

'To know whether you are enjoying a piece of music or not', wrote Samuel Butler in 1890, 'you must see whether you find yourself looking at the advertisement for Pear's Soap at the end of the programme book.'

Why does one switch off like this? And yet, on other occasions, when one is tired and not in the mood for listening to music, why does one find the performance compelling and wish that time could stand still? The answer lies in the performer's artistry – that elusive, almost magical quality which is the hallmark of all great musicians, and transcends the boundaries of age, class, language and race. Without that elusive, magical quality, no performer can make the listener listen.

Alfred Neuhaus asks: 'What must be done to make a performance live? Is it patience, work, suffering, joy, self-sacrifice?' He says: 'It is to play our magnificent piano literature in such a way as to make the hearer like it, to make him love life still more, make his feeling more intense, his longings more acute and give greater depth to his understanding'. The performance is the culminating experience of an artist's intensive work. Something extra happens during a performance which never happens during one's practice. A performance compels continuity, courage and greater concentration. An audience is necessary to give the performer that vital inspiration and spontaneity. Rubinstein said that each audience stimulated him afresh, no matter how familiar were the works he was playing – and indeed one of the unique qualities of his playing was always his spontaneity.

Alan Schulmann, a cellist in the NBC orchestra, talking about one of the greatest teachers of the past, Toscanini, epitomizes what I feel about music and its performance: 'When I think of Toscanini's performances, I think of the clarity of texture, architectural unity, his linear sense; his phrases were marvellous arcs. I think of the flexibility, the forward motion, and yet the repose. The ability to milk every note of the phrase with Italian warmth, intelligence and good taste. *And* the electrifying, incisive rhythm. Yet none of the musicians I knew, or who wrote about him could describe the final magic of his performances. He relied on his innate musical sense – "Cantare, non solfeggiare", that is "Sing, don't play exercises".'

This magic cannot be taught but only stimulated. I advise all aspiring performers to develop a wide appreciation of the Arts in general, to listen to as many live performances as possible, to study folk-songs of many cultures, to take part in chamber music and accompany other musicians, to sing in a choir, be an active listener in the concert hall, and to learn also to absorb the sights and sounds of everyday life.

Listening to birdsong helps one to understand the sound of many of Beethoven's trills. Messiaen, too, has recorded birdsong and uses it in his music. Bartók was influenced by the sounds of insects in the night. Listen to the rhythmic beat of the wheels of a train – the triplet rhythm done to perfection; feel the lilt of a swing – 6/8 rhythm; observe the to-ing and fro-ing of waves on the shore – directly invoked in such music as Debussy's *L'Isle joyeuse* and *La Mer*; savour the silence of night . . . all these, recalled at the right moment, will perhaps help to illumine otherwise routine playing.

Something makes people want to perform. I would never urge anyone on to the concert platform who does not wish to be there, and no teacher ever should. But for those who want to perform, the only way to learn the job is to do it. What the teacher must do is to help in creating the most favourable conditions for individual artistry to emerge and flourish. Many aspects of the essential groundwork have been mentioned, and the teacher must always be prepared to help the aspiring performer on the practical details of giving a recital (some general tips are included in the Appendix following).

What qualities must a musician possess in order to become a great performer? I would answer only half jestingly: First, you must have inclination and imagination, backed up by application, concentration and determination. There will be perspiration and at times frustration, even tribulation. But with inspiration you will receive appreciation, ovations and adulation!

Looking back over my years of teaching and to the many young talents entrusted to me, I am deeply grateful to them. For they have taught me as much as I have taught them.

Appendix: Giving a Recital

Before the date: (1) Open a file labelled with the place and date of the recital, and keep in it all correspondence and details of the engagement. (2) Inquire about the size of the hall and its acoustics; make, size and condition of the piano; the type of audience, and the length of the programme required. Decide on your programme with these details in mind. Remember (a) to include pieces of lighthearted charm and wit, and (b) to prepare an encore. (3) Send promptly all information required by the organisers – programme details, biographical note, photograph, etc. (4) Make certain you have enough time booked for rehearsal in the hall. (5) Organise a page-turner, if required. (6) Plan your travelling time-table carefully, allowing for possible transport delays and time to recover after the journey. (7) Check dress requirements – lounge suit, dinner jacket or tails (with correct tie!) for men; long or short dress for women. (8) Prepare a check-list of items to take with you. Don't forget the concert-file, paper handkerchiefs, nail-file, spare spectacles, flask of coffee, tea or fruit juice for interval and (in winter) gloves or hand warmer.

On the day: (1) Be punctual for rehearsal and performance. Never leave anything till the last minute, so that you avoid panic and the consequent frayed nerves. (2) Never take drugs or alcohol to calm pre-concert nerves; learn to live with them. (3) Do not alter your usual pre-concert eating habits. (4) Don't change your programme except for the most compelling reasons. (5) Rehearse the full range of items in your programme to familiarize yourself with the instrument and the acoustics of the hall. (6) Awkward turns and repeats should be rehearsed with a page-turner, if you have one. (7)

Before the concert, practise 'key' passages slowly in the Artist's Room to keep the hands supple. (8) Never leave valuables unattended in the Artist's Room.

On the platform: (1) Try to achieve a rapport with your audience as quickly as possible. A ready, natural smile is a great asset. (2) Walk on to the platform steadily and walk off swiftly. Notice at the rehearsal any awkward access to avoid tripping up. (3) Check that the stool is at the right height and does not wobble. (4) Take your time. Do not play before you and the audience are ready. Wait for silence before you begin. (5) Never stamp on the floor or bang on the pedals. Sit as straight as possible and do not fidget, snort or pull faces. (6) If you have a memory slip, try to conceal it and 'vamp' till you recover. Avoid at all costs having to stop and apologise.

After the recital: (1) Be diplomatic. If you are disappointed with the piano or with audience reaction, do not say so. These can be sensitive areas with concert organizers. (2) Be courteous. Write a letter of appreciation after your visit, especially if you have received any hospitality. (3) Everyone gets both good and bad reviews. Do not be depressed by the latter: it is only one person's opinion. (4) Don't rest on your laurels – keep on working!